THE LITTLE

MAN UNITED

THIRD EDITION
Unofficial and unauthorised

EDITED BY
JUSTYN BARNES

CARLTON
BOOKS

First published by Carlton Books in 2001
Reprinted with updates in 2004, 2006, 2008
Second edition 2010
Third edition 2014

Carlton Books Limited
20 Mortimer Street
London W1T 3JW

A CIP catalogue record of this book is available from the British Library.

ISBN 978-1-78097-587-0

Printed in Dubai

CONTENTS

INTRODUCTION 5

CHAPTER 1: THE UNITED WAY **6**

CHAPTER 2: HEROES OF THE SHIRT **36**

CHAPTER 3: GAFFER TALK **90**

CHAPTER 4: INTO EUROPE **112**

CHAPTER 5: MAGIC MOMENTS **130**

CHAPTER 6: FERGIE'S SAYINGS **146**

CHAPTER 7: THE GLORY DAYS **180**

INTRODUCTION

Football, someone said, is all about opinions. And one club generates more opinions than most. Whether it's in the media, the dressing room or in the pub, Manchester United is frequently the topic of conversation. Hardly surprising really, when you consider that many of the game's most dramatic events, finest players and greatest matches have United at their core.

So here is a collection of some of the best soundbites around, covering all that's legendary about the club – the glory of the 1968 European Cup win, the class of '92, the incomparable achievements of Sir Alex Ferguson and the appointment of David Moyes. Best, Charlton, Giggsy, Becks, Keano, Cantona, Ferguson, Rooney and now van Persie and Mata are all featured, along with the thoughts of a host of other legends from across the decades. Whether it's to give praise or show warmth, jealousy or regret, everyone's talking about United.

CHAPTER 1

THE UNITED WAY

" For men who work on the shop floor, the one highlight of their week is to go and watch football. Matt Busby used to say you should give that man something he can't do himself, something exciting. That's why Manchester United always play attacking football. **"**

SIR BOBBY CHARLTON

"I had always had a feeling that one day I would join United. I don't know whether it was wishful thinking or just a sixth sense about my destiny.**"**

DENIS LAW

> **"** I'm in love with Manchester United. It is like finding a wife who has given me the perfect marriage. **"**

ERIC CANTONA

❝Fourteen years ago, on the day of a youth team match I'd go to the pub with my dad and brother to have chicken and chips in a basket. Nowadays, I wouldn't go near a chip even two days before a game!**❞**

GARY NEVILLE

April 2006

" Arriving at Old Trafford is moving to the highest level – there is nowhere else to go now. **"**

MICHAEL CARRICK

July 2006

" At the end of the game you're knackered and there are times when you come out of the shower when you feel you can hardly walk. But if I came off the pitch and didn't feel like that, I'd feel as if I'd cheated myself by not running my hardest. **"**

WAYNE ROONEY

on giving his all, 2006

"When I see the rain it isn't important to me now. If I go outside and it rains, I jog! I smile, I say, 'Welcome to England!' At first I would be angry, now I make a joke about it. When it rains, I dance!**"**

PATRICE EVRA

gets acclimatised to the Manchester weather, November 2006

❝David Beckham and I were standing in the centre-circle when the crowd started calling me names. I said to him, 'I suppose you're used to all this.' He grinned and replied, 'Yeah, but in my case, it's not true!'**❞**

Referee **GRAHAM POLL**

"I was beginning to get worried. I've never gone three seasons without winning the title before.**"**

RYAN GIGGS

2007

❝I was never fined for the Sharpey Shuffle, but the Boss threatened to. I said if he stopped me doing it I would stop scoring goals!**❞**

LEE SHARPE's

unique goal celebrations didn't impress Alex Ferguson

❝My wife told me that I loved Manchester United more than her. I told her that I loved Manchester City more than her...**❞**

An unnamed **MEMBER OF THE CARRICKFERGUS BRANCH OF THE SUPPORTERS' CLUB**
explains why his marriage ended in divorce

“When I was eighteen, nineteen, I went down to join the Welsh squad a couple of times with a bit of a beard. They started calling me 'George' from then on, and the name's stuck!**”**

RYAN GIGGS

"I'm not one for falling over easily.
I'm not one for diving in the penalty box.
I don't think the team has ever got any
penalties from me. **"**

United's very honest striker **ANDREW COLE**

"My dad tells me that I've always wanted to play here. He said when I first saw Old Trafford I just stood and stared for an hour.**"**

GARY NEVILLE

❝I found it very difficult returning to Old Trafford for the first time. I got a marvellous reception, but the game just passed me by. Some of the Chelsea lads had a go at me after we scored. They reckoned I didn't jump up and down enough.**❞**

MARK HUGHES

"I love pleasing United fans, but I also get a kick out of being on the pitch and having the power to aggravate thousands of opposing fans without them being able to do anything about it.**"**

MARK HUGHES

❝Here, it's all about the next challenge. No matter what we've done, no matter how big the game we've won, the boss just says we can celebrate what we've done to win a trophy – but the next day it's forgotten.**❞**

Onwards and upwards for **NEMANJA VIDIC**
May 2008

❝ There's no amount of money that can buy the feeling we have now. We want more. We want to go past people who have been here before, we want to win two, three, if we can. That's what drives us on. **❞**

RIO FERDINAND

on United's desire for more Champions League glory, May 2009

" We had fights, and I mean punch-ups, every day. But it didn't matter. We were men enough to take it and forget about it come kick-off time. It didn't matter whether Nobby had chinned Denis or Denis had chinned Bill Foulkes, we were all aiming for the same thing ultimately… **"**

GEORGE BEST

" … and by matchday,
you had to be friends because
there was only one bath! **"**

GEORGE BEST

❝You go to any factory or office and not everyone is going to like each other. Of course, you are going to have clashes. It's not to say we won't have a good do at Christmas and come Saturday, we will all want to win and we will help each other out.**❞**

ROY KEANE

" As YTS players, we were all assigned to clean someone's boots. I got Eric Cantona which I was well pleased with … although Brian McClair was the biggest tipper! **"**

WES BROWN

"We all agree, Jaap Stam is harder than Arnie! **"**

UNITED FANS'

chant at Sturm Graz's Arnold Schwarzenegger Stadium,
December 2000

❝David is a good friend, but it's no different to when Eric Cantona or Bryan Robson left. Manchester United will move on, as we have in the past. Inside the club, we have already moved on.**❞**

PHIL NEVILLE

on life after Becks, July 2003

"Bigger players than David have left in the past and will leave in the future. But the spirit will stay in the team because we still have a big group of players here who remain the heartbeat of the team.**"**

NICKY BUTT

" When you're in the tunnel and you hear on the speakers: 'Please welcome the champions of England, the champions of Europe and the champions of the world,' you just believe that you're going to crush anybody that is in your way. I get goosebumps every time I walk out at Old Trafford. **"**

DIMITAR BERBATOV

January 2009

❝When I knew about the bid from United there was only one place I was going to go. The players here are unbelievable, the club has fans all over the world and hopefully I can do well.**❞**

WAYNE ROONEY

joins for £27million in summer 2004

"I have been here since I was
a young boy and I have grown very fond of
the club and the fans, they have been an
integral part of my life.**"**

RYAN GIGGS

CHAPTER 2

HEROES OF THE SHIRT

"Perhaps I should be an example to people, but I do not think that way, I do not react that way. I am simply me.**"**

ERIC CANTONA

"I don't know about making referees professional. They love themselves enough as it is now.**"**

PAUL SCHOLES

"I find it amusing that Roy Keane has this really hard image. Once you get to know him, he's not as bad as he's portrayed. I like to chat with him. He is what he is and I like that.**"**

DWIGHT YORKE

" Roy Keane is Damien, the devil incarnate off the film *The Omen*. He's evil. Even in training. **"**

RYAN GIGGS

" I'm moody and grumpy
most of the time. **"**

ROY KEANE

If I thought personal glory was more important than team glory, I would have taken up an individual sport.

ERIC CANTONA

"It wasn't my choice to become a goalkeeper, but I was probably too violent to play outfield.**"**

PETER SCHMEICHEL

❝I find it natural to score goals.
When I head towards goal, I know exactly
what to do. **❞**

OLE GUNNAR SOLSKJAER

*then an almost unknown Norwegian striker, speaking soon after he
signed for United in 1996 – he wasn't exaggerating*

❝If I had to pick a weakness in Beckham's game it's his left foot. But that's like saying Maradona's right foot wasn't too clever.**❞**

GEORGE BEST

"You need to get the balance right. You have to take it seriously because it's your job and you're paid to win things, but you should enjoy each moment because there will come a time when you won't be able to play football again.**"**

DWIGHT YORKE

"There's quite a few funny sights in the dressing room, but the thing that makes me happiest is Yorkie's smile. It makes everyone else smile too!**"**

OLE GUNNAR SOLSKJAER

on the ray of sunshine that was his fellow striker Dwight Yorke

❝In the changing room, Keaney would say, 'Watch this,' and he'd start humming or singing a song near Gary Pallister. Five minutes later, Pally would be singing the same song. It never failed, that one.**❞**

RYAN GIGGS

" Fabien Barthez is a fantastic character. Once he came into the office and told me he needed a woman to take care of him. What he really meant was that he needed a housekeeper! **"**

LYN LAFFIN

Sir Alex's P.A., also looks after the players

"We all make an extra effort for the foreign players to make them feel comfortable… Having said that, if they're not working hard enough they get shouted at!**"**

ROY KEANE

"It's a panic buy.**"**

Former Liverpool captain **EMLYN HUGHES**
when United bought Eric Cantona

"It's not a case of signing autographs so that people will think I'm a nice guy, but rather that I don't want them to have a bad experience. I don't want to hurt them by letting them down. **"**

ERIC CANTONA

“When you see Eric Cantona brushing up
his skills, you know that no-one can be
satisfied with their standard. **”**

RYAN GIGGS

"I don't really like the attention from girls – apart from anything else I already have a girlfriend. I like supporters of football whatever sex they are, but it's not so great when you're on a night-out and girls just sit next to you… but to be honest it doesn't happen to me that often anyway.**"**

GARY NEVILLE

October 1996

"You shouldn't be nuts, but it doesn't matter if you are a bit peculiar.**"**

PETER SCHMEICHEL

identifies the essential quality of a goalkeeper

I'm sure Arsenal fans are working on some new chants, but they can sing what they like. I've got three nice medals to show them.

Ex-Spurs striker **TEDDY SHERINGHAM**
looks forward to his next match against Arsenal in
summer 1999 soon after winning the Treble

❝I play with a certain passion and fire. I have to accept that sometimes this fire does harm.**❞**

ERIC CANTONA

before the infamous kung-fu incident at Selhurst Park

in January 1995

"Certainly take the advice of others but always, always be yourself. **"**

ERIC CANTONA

"Who am I more scared of – the gaffer or my missus? Neither. Always have your alibi ready – that's my motto!**"**

ROY KEANE

❝When I do quit football, it'll be at the top. I certainly wouldn't contemplate playing for teams that are any less successful than Manchester United or playing for the reserves. Once I feel I'm not at the top any more, I'll quit. **❞**

ERIC CANTONA

talking in the summer of 1996, a year before he retired

❝In 30 or 40 years time, I'll probably boast about having played with Eric… Even before I came to the club I looked up to him and admired his skills. And I admire him even more now after I've trained with him and got to know him as a person. He was a huge influence at the club and gave everybody a lift with his presence. That is probably what I'll miss most of all. **❞**

OLE GUNNAR SOLSKJAER

on hearing of Eric Cantona's retirement, summer 1997

“I think the fans appreciate my attitude, and I'd like to think there's no crap about me. What you see is what you get.**”**

ROY KEANE

" Paul Scholes is probably the most complete player at United. He is the type of player I like, someone with special abilities. I wouldn't know who to compare him with. **"**

Scholes' former team-mate **JORDI CRUYFF**

"Nobody's going to tell me I'm the world's best, but no-one's going to tell me I'm a crap footballer either. I have belief in myself, simple as that. **"**

TEDDY SHERINGHAM

❝Teddy has always been a thinking man's player, like Franz Beckenbauer and Bobby Moore.**❞**

GEORGE BEST

"A lot of the lads here have nice cars, but they're young and they're single and you can't take the money with you. I've never seen a coffin with pockets.**"**

ROY KEANE

❝ The fans were singing my song for ages and I was like, 'Oh my God!' The buzz it gave me was incredible. **❞**

Young star **JOHN O'SHEA**
enjoys a crowd rendition of "When Johnny goes marching down the wing, O'Shea, O'Shea"

"My goal for this year is to become the complete striker. **"**

RUUD VAN NISTELROOY's

undemanding 2003 New Year's resolution!

❝The variety of Van Nistelrooy's goals is incredible. If a cross comes in you know he'll be on the end of it, but he's also capable of picking the ball up 40 yards out and scoring. Phenomenal.**❞**

GEORGE BEST

❝I feel really sad about leaving but I have to move on. I've always been a United fan and will always follow the team.**❞**

DAVID BECKHAM

June 2003

"Anyone who knows me will tell you I'm not flash. I'm just a normal kind of guy who happens to play football. I think fans can see if people are flash and we haven't got one flash person in our squad.**"**

RIO FERDINAND

"You look around the Nike HQ and see people like Michael Jordan and Tiger Woods have buildings named after them. That's what I want – Ferdinand Towers in my honour! I want to join the legends.**"**

RIO FERDINAND

"Rooney can be the best in the world at 25 if he knows you need to train hard, go to bed early and be careful what you eat.**"**

ERIC CANTONA

❝The fans will be upset because they loved him. He was a great leader. The best thing about Roy Keane is that you knew where you stood with him.**❞**

DAVID BECKHAM

on Roy Keane's departure from Old Trafford in November 2005

❝ I'm very proud to have scored 100 goals for United. **❞**

RUUD VAN NISTELROOY

reaches his ton at Everton in February 2004, after just 131 games

❝ After Philip left, I had half an hour to myself driving in my car and I did think: 'This isn't going to last forever. I'd better enjoy this.' **❞**

GARY NEVILLE

on life at Old Trafford after brother
Phil joined Everton in the summer of 2005

"Maybe in the future I could return.**"**

CRISTIANO RONALDO

*doesn't rule out a return to Old Trafford after
joining Real Madrid, February 2010*

❝He started in 1992 and where are we now, 2009? Jesus. To play at the level he has been doing, he has to be the greatest ever player in the Premier League. Not just because of his longevity, but because he is still playing for Manchester United and still getting man-of-the-match awards.**❞**

STEVE BRUCE

on Ryan Giggs, December 2009

“He has made a fantastic contribution to our season. In terms of impact he has had as big an impact as anyone I can imagine.**”**

SIR ALEX FERGUSON

on Robin van Persie's efforts during the 2012–13 season

" Patrice is one of the finest leaders around the dressing room that I have ever seen. **"**

DAVID MOYES

assesses Patrice Evra, December 2013

" He is a boy who continually gets better in the games he plays. It doesn't really seem to affect him in a way it does others. **"**

DAVID MOYES

on Wayne Rooney's spirit, November 2013

❝Vida is probably the best centre-half I have ever worked with. He is that good, he really is.**❞**

DAVID MOYES

sings the praises of Nemanja Vidic, September 2013

"I wanted to go to a place where I would feel happy and I'm happy now. Manchester United are a massive club, with the most fans around the world so it's a big challenge for my career, a big step.**"**

JUAN MATA

joins from Chelsea, January 2014

66 When you have to make a hard decision in your life, I always listen to that little boy inside me. What does he want? That boy was screaming for Manchester United. **99**

ROBIN VAN PERSIE

explains why he left Arsenal

"All these guys here know how to win and become champions."

ROBIN VAN PERSIE

evaluates his Manchester United team-mates

"As soon as you get the ball I am going to be in your face. You are not going to like it one bit. Are you ready for that because that's what's going to happen.**"**

DARREN FLETCHER

on his attitude in midfield

❝Everybody can see what a player we have on our hands.**❞**

DAVID MOYES

praises Adnan Januzaj, January 2014

❝You cannot turn down the chance to join Manchester United. ❞

JUAN MATA

after leaving London for Manchester in January 2014

CHAPTER 3

GAFFER TALK

" When you look down the list of who you are going to get points off, you mark Manchester United down as zero. **"**

Derby County manager **JIM SMITH**

❝I don't look at Manchester United. They've got 70,000 gates; they've got the Beckhams and so on, all young and hungry. My dream is to become second best – only then will I start worrying about the freaks from across the Pennines!**❞**

Leeds United manager **DAVID O'LEARY**

"You have to give Fergie credit. He has brought United on leaps and bounds… the bastard! **"**

Liverpool manager **ROY EVANS**

February 1998

" For the first year I was a pro, when the manager walked into the room I just shut up and sat up as if I was at school. If I heard him coming down the stairs, I would turn around and go back into the dressing room. I was definitely scared of him. **"**

PHIL NEVILLE

on Sir Alex Ferguson

“People don't see him when he comes in and pinches our chocolates, or when he sings to us! The manager thinks he's got an excellent singing voice and well… we always agree with the manager.**”**

LYN LAFFIN

Sir Alex's P.A., relates another side to the gaffer's character

"Matt Busby liked a joke. Could he tell a joke? Could he hell! He'd get the punchline half-right and I'd say what it should have been. He'd reply, 'That's what I meant', and I'd roar…**"**

JIMMY TARBUCK

❝He treated my dad with a lot of respect and always took time out for him.
I mean, little things are important to us and Matt even remembered what sort of sandwiches my dad liked.**❞**

GEORGE BEST

on Sir Matt Busby

"We had a few problems with the wee fella, but I prefer to remember his genius.**"**

SIR MATT BUSBY

on George Best

❝Eric Cantona is a great player, but he is not as good as Ryan Giggs.❞

PETER SWALES

former Manchester City chairman

" Ryan Giggs is the detonator,
the man who can make
Manchester United explode. **"**

Former Fulham manager **JEAN TIGANA**

The manager doesn't want me to live like a monk. If he tried to make me live like a monk my football would go down the drain. He understands that, we've had that conversation.

Ladies' man **DWIGHT YORKE**

"They should have brought
in the ten-yard rule years ago.
If Schmeichel was in goal and the ball was
moved forward because one of his
defenders was arguing with the referee, he'd
have come out and smacked them because
his goal's at threat.**"**

GORDON STRACHAN

"Everybody now talks about Cantona being the main catalyst of United's latter-day glories. But without Bryan Robson, I maintain United might not have had the same stature when Eric arrived. Robson was the essence of United.**"**

RON ATKINSON

"United haven't done anything special this season."

ARSENE WENGER

the week before United beat Arsenal 6–1 in the 2000–01 Premiership

❝This team never loses.
They just run out of time.**❞**

United coach **STEVE McCLAREN**

"Unfortunately it was a very bad bottle of wine and he was complaining, so when we go to Old Trafford for the second leg, on my birthday, I will take a beautiful bottle of Portuguese wine.**"**

JOSE MOURINHO

on his post-match tipple with Sir Alex

❝I've got more respect for Ferguson than anyone else in the game. He is the master. He's like a Scouser, really. He's funny, and he even votes Labour. I love him.❞

JAMIE CARRAGHER

September 2008

❝I want to build an exciting team. That's always the way I've wanted my football to be played and I've not known it any other way.**❞**

DAVID MOYES'

footballing philosophy, January 2014

"The amount of big players wanting to join United is incredible. Maybe players want to go for the money to other clubs but if you ask them where they really want to be they want to wear the badge of Manchester United. **"**

DAVID MOYES

January 2014

"So come on David Moyes!
Play like Fergie's boys!
We'll go wild, wild, wild! **"**

THE STRETFORD END

sing for David Moyes, to the tune of Slade's Cum on Feel the Noize

CHAPTER 4

INTO EUROPE

"I want our fans to be happy and for them to enjoy the experience of being at Old Trafford. I would appeal to them to just enjoy the performance we intend to put on for them.**"**

Opposing captain **FRANCESCO TOTTI**
shortly before his AS Roma side lost 7–1 in the
UEFA Champions League, April 2007

" Winning the European Cup in 1968 was a big thank you to the players that weren't with us, and even those of us who did survive. That night was something special. Everyone in the world wanted us to win at Wembley and doing so was part of the history – it was important the club managed it. **"**

SIR BOBBY CHARLTON

reflects on United's European Cup victory
under Sir Matt Busby in 1968, March 2008

"For me, personally, I've had three European finals when it tipped down with rain, so when the rain came in Moscow I said, 'This will do for me; this will do.' I was delighted to see it and with [John] Terry slipping… you know, it's amazing. Luck's luck, and you can't win without it.**"**

SIR ALEX FERGUSON

in Moscow after lifting the Champions League trophy in 2008

❝I couldn't tell you which hotel we stayed at, whether we had a post-match banquet… it's just a blank. But the game itself, I can remember almost every kick. I was fortunate enough to score in the Final. I remember the ball being cleared and coming to me. And I knew I was going to score, I just knew.**❞**

GEORGE BEST

on the 1968 European Cup Final victory

"It was an unbelievable night. I watched football as a kid and saw players go up to the Royal Box at Wembley and thought, 'What are they crying for?' But as soon as the final whistle went, I just sunk to my knees. I couldn't stop myself.**"**

RYAN GIGGS

on the 1999 UEFA Champions League Final win

" The last time I saw a person dance on a table was Giggsy after we won the European Cup. He fell off and everyone was a bit worried, but he just got straight back on the table and carried on! **"**

TEDDY SHERINGHAM

"Teddy Sheringham did all the hard work for me and I just managed to get a toe on the ball to steer it in. I have never had a better feeling than that and I doubt I ever will. It'll take a couple of years to sink in.**"**

OLE GUNNAR SOLSKJAER

on scoring the winning the goal in the
1999 UEFA Champions League Final

" Even though it was the last minute, I was quite calm. I just knew we'd score, I really did. And as soon as we equalised I knew that there was only one team that could win it. I could see that Munich were gone. **"**

Suspended captain **ROY KEANE's**
view from the bench

❝When I went down on my knees
I strained my ligaments and I was
out for the whole summer. **❞**

OLE GUNNAR SOLSKJAER

reveals the cost of his UEFA Champions League
Final-winning goal celebrations

❝ At the end of this game, the European Cup will be only six feet away from you, and you'll not even able to touch it if we lose. And for many of you, that will be the closest you will ever get. Don't you dare come back in here without giving your all. **❞**

SIR ALEX FERGUSON's

half-time team-talk during the 1999 UEFA Champions League Final against Bayern Munich

❝ February 6, 1958, was a black day in the history of Manchester United, but also for football in general. I'm proud to be a fan of Manchester United. People in England say, 'God save the Queen'. Today, I say, 'God save Manchester United.' **❞**

BAYERN MUNICH CHAIRMAN
at the service to commemorate the Munich Tragedy,
February 2008

" Even today when I see archive films of Duncan Edwards it really upsets me. We'll never get over Munich. The mood in the city was ghastly… The whole country felt for the club. Even in the 1958 Cup Final, everyone was on Manchester United's side… a bit different from today. **"**

NORMAN WILLIAMS

United supporter

❝We used to go here, there and everywhere in groups, loads of us. We went to Butlins together, as a youth side we had our first trip abroad to Switzerland together. We were pals, best pals… and then the crash happened.**❞**

'Busby Babe' **WILF McGUINESS**,
who missed the fateful trip to Red Star Belgrade through injury

❝I can still remember the first television pictures. Snow falling in the darkness, the flakes illuminated by camera lighting and the sudden burst of flashbulbs. Snow, twisted metal, seats which had been hurled from the aircraft, overcoats and odd shoes.**❞**

TOM TYRRELL

sportswriter and United fan

❝I was having a shave in the kitchen when my wife shouted out from the front room, 'Have you heard the news?' I'd shaved half of my face, but I don't think I shaved the other half for three days. I was absolutely devastated.**❞**

HAROLD WOOD

club steward

"It may seem odd but when
I think of Manchester United I think of
Roger Byrne, Duncan Edwards and Eddie
Colman before the Munich aircrash, and of
Harry Gregg, Bill Foulkes and Nobby Stiles
afterwards. Best, Law and Crerand were
replaceable somehow. They weren't the heart
of the team.**"**

SIR BOBBY CHARLTON

CHAPTER 5

MAGIC MOMENTS

"Sir Matt Busby came into the dressing room after we'd become champions. He said very little but his expression said it all. His beloved Manchester United were back on top.**"**

BRYAN ROBSON

on the end of the 26-year wait for a League Championship victory

"I can't believe it, I actually scored!
My first goal in 90 League and cup games!
Strangely, Ole Gunnar Solskjaer had a
premonition I was going to do it.
He came up to me three times in the hour
before kick-off and said, 'You're going to
score today, Phil. Remember what I say.'
I just laughed.**"**

PHIL NEVILLE

on his winning goal against Chelsea on 28 February 1998

❝Well, I rose like a salmon at the far post, but Pally rose like a fresher salmon and towered above me, headed the ball at the keeper, the keeper fumbled, then I saw a sudden flash of brilliant red and leathered it into the roof of the net with my left foot sponsored by Diadora boots. **❞**

DAVID MAY's

vivid description of his goal in United's 4–0 thrashing of Porto in March 1997

134

❝It got to the point where I just thought, 'I'm going to take everyone on.' And when I got through I just hit it as hard as I could. David Seaman got a lot of stick, but it really was the only place I could have put it to beat him. **❞**

RYAN GIGGS

describing his wonder goal in the 1999 FA Cup semi-final replay against Arsenal

"Ryan's goal was meant to be. A higher power was at work.**"**

Arsenal defender **TONY ADAMS**

❝Ryan just put his head down, ran like he always does, didn't pass and got lucky.**❞**

NICKY BUTT's

view of Giggs' goal

"After the 1994 FA Cup Final, I just sank to the floor and all my emotions poured out. There were tears, I cried. But there's nothing wrong with that.**"**

PETER SCHMEICHEL

remembers United's 1994 Double triumph

❝ When the seagulls follow the trawler, it is because they think sardines will be thrown into the sea. Merci. **❞**

ERIC CANTONA's

enigmatic utterance after his court case in March 1995

“The seagulls following the boat represent Cantona's fans and the press who are always pursuing him. The trawler is a symbol of the judicial system which almost incarcerated him. The sardines represent Cantona himself, and the other players, who feel they are products in the capitalist system and world of sport. **”**

French literature professor **RUFUS DOISNEAU**
offers an explanation

❝My lawyer wanted me to talk.
I could have said, 'The curtains are
pink but I love them.' **❞**

ERIC CANTONA

offers an alternative explanation

"You couldn't have asked much more of a man who was under the most intense pressure, but he appeared about as relaxed as someone wandering down to the local shops for a pint of milk.**"**

ALAN HANSEN

on Eric's comeback game against Liverpool on 1 October 1995

" It got the team spirit going, that's for sure. He's come back from what I thought was a very severe punishment. Some fans go a bit far and I think a lot of players would like to do what Eric did. There's been a lot said about the bloke in the stand that night and, fair enough, maybe he didn't deserve a size 12 boot in the throat, but some fans are really bad. Anyway, Eric got his punishment, did his time and that's the end of it. **"**

ROY KEANE

December 1996

"For pure ability and talent, player for player, this is the best United team I've played in. And it can get better. We are champions now and that gives you an extra bit of confidence.**"**

RYAN GIGGS

looks ahead after winning his eighth Premiership winners' medal

❝It has been a great honour and privilege for me to play for Manchester United for over 12 years… in front of the best supporters in the world.**❞**

ROY KEANE

says goodbye

CHAPTER 6

FERGIE'S SAYINGS

"The afternoon of 2 May 1993, when we were crowned the champions of England was the day I truly became the manager of Manchester United. Until that fancy bit of silverware was in our grasp, nothing could be taken for granted. **"**

SIR ALEX FERGUSON

"Nicky Butt's a real Manchester boy.
A bit of a scallywag. He comes from Gorton
where it is said they take the pavements in of
a night time.**"**

SIR ALEX FERGUSON

❝If he's got a temperament, wait until he sees my temperament. **❞**

SIR ALEX FERGUSON

wasn't frightened of Eric Cantona's reputation
when he signed him in November 1992

" Some of the players call me 'Gaffer' …
and when Gary Pallister wants to take a
weekend off, he calls me 'God'! **"**

SIR ALEX FERGUSON

December 1995

"I've sung every song in the world in the bath. I'm thinking of releasing a CD called *Singalong with Fergie!* **"**

SIR ALEX "PAVAROTTI" FERGUSON

"The intense pride in their city has made a deep impression on me and I now regard myself as an adopted Mancunian.**"**

SIR ALEX FERGUSON

on being awarded the Freedom of the City of Manchester

"My wife's always saying, 'Why don't you grow up?' and I say, 'Why should I? I'm enjoying myself being silly and young!'**"**

SIR ALEX FERGUSON

❝Eric Cantona is the best prepared footballer I've ever had. He's first at the training ground, he does his own warm-up and then he does ours. He trains brilliantly and then he practises after training and he's the last to leave the car park, signing autographs. He's happy to do hospital visits whenever you ask him to do anything. He's a model pro, an absolute dream footballer.**❞**

SIR ALEX FERGUSON

❝Managing this club can become an obsession. **❞**

SIR ALEX FERGUSON

❝I remember Viv Anderson saying to me once: 'You're off your head being a manager. I wouldn't be a manager in a million years.' When he took the Barnsley job in 1993, his first phone call was from me. I said: 'Welcome to the madhouse!'**❞**

SIR ALEX FERGUSON

❝I don't think any player in the history of football will get the sentence he got – unless they had killed Bert Millichip's dog.**❞**

SIR ALEX FERGUSON

slams Eric Cantona's nine-month ban

(Millichip was Football Association Chairman at the time)

How would I be without all this, please tell me? And my wife wouldn't let me retire. Shc kicks me out at seven every morning. She's quite a formidable person.

SIR ALEX FERGUSON

doesn't consider retiring in 2008

" Everyone has done so well, I'm beginning to dread picking the team. **"**

SIR ALEX FERGUSON

ahead of the visit of Everton in January 2009

"I've known David since he was 11 and it's been a pleasure to see him grow and develop into the player he has become. I wish him and his family every success in the future and thank him for his service to the club.**"**

SIR ALEX FERGUSON

"Yes, we take terrible risks, but there's always a chance we'll win the match.**"**

SIR ALEX FERGUSON

April 2009

❝This club has always had players who show their true colours when the going gets tough dating back to the era of Nobby Stiles, Paddy Crerand and Bobby Charlton through to players like Bryan Robson, Mark Hughes, Steve Bruce and on to today's crop of monsters! That is why Manchester United have had so much success.**❞**

SIR ALEX FERGUSON

reflects on United's amazing 2002–03 Premiership title triumph

"Roy Keane has been a fantastic servant for Manchester United. The best midfield player in the world of his generation, he is already one of the great figures in our club's illustrious history.**"**

SIR ALEX FERGUSON

on Keano

"His whole meaning of life is about Manchester United. **"**

SIR ALEX FERGUSON

on captain Gary Neville

“Some believe the greatest courage in football is the courage to win the ball. The other kind of courage – and it's a moral courage – is the courage to keep the ball. That's what Ronaldo has. All the great players had it. Best had it, Charlton had it, Cantona. 'I'll take the kick, I'll take the injury. But I'll keep the ball. I'll beat the bully.'**”**

SIR ALEX FERGUSON

on Cristiano Ronaldo, October 2008

❝ Football, eh! Bloody hell! **❞**

SIR ALEX FERGUSON

in the tunnel minutes after United's last-gasp
UEFA Champions League Final win in May 1999

"I remember the first time I saw him. He was 13 and just floated over the ground like a cocker spaniel chasing a piece of silver paper in the wind. **"**

SIR ALEX FERGUSON's

first impressions of Ryan Giggs

"It's getting tickly now – squeaky-bum time, I call it.**"**

SIR ALEX FERGUSON

on the title run-in with Arsenal, 2003

❝My greatest challenge is not what is happening right at this moment, my greatest challenge was knocking Liverpool right off their perch. And you can print that.**❞**

SIR ALEX FERGUSON
on where his priorities lay, 2002

❝Myths grow all the time. If I was to listen to the number of times I've thrown teacups then we've gone through some crockery in this place. It's completely exaggerated, but I don't like people arguing back with me.**❞**

SIR ALEX FERGUSON

on his notorious "hairdryer" treatment

If If my parents were still alive, they would be very proud. They gave me a good start in life, the values that have driven me, and the confidence to believe in myself. **JJ**

SIR ALEX FERGUSON's

family roots

“ Do you think I would enter into a contract with that mob? Absolutely no chance. I would not sell them a virus. That is a 'No' by the way. There is no agreement whatsoever between the clubs. **”**

SIR ALEX FERGUSON

on Real Madrid's attempts to buy Cristiano Ronaldo, December 2008

"Sometimes you have a noisy neighbour. You cannot do anything about that. They will always be noisy. You just have to get on with your life, put your television on and turn it up a bit louder. Today the players showed their form. That is the best answer of all.**"**

SIR ALEX FERGUSON

after beating City 4–3, September 2009

❝It's City isn't it? They are a small club, with a small mentality. All they can talk about is Manchester United, that's all they've done and they can't get away from it.**❞**

SIR ALEX FERGUSON

on Manchester City's Carlos Tevez poster

"Sometimes you look in a field and you see a cow and you think it's a better cow than the one you've got in your own field. It's a fact. Right? And it never really works out that way.**"**

SIR ALEX FERGUSON

on Wayne Rooney's transfer request, 2010

"There obviously will be a point
when I do quit and when it is I absolutely
have no idea because I tried that, and
it was an absolute disaster.**"**

SIR ALEX FERGUSON

on retirement, 2010

❝It'll take them a century to get to our level of history.**❞**

SIR ALEX FERGUSON

on Manchester City, May 2012

" The decision to retire is one that I have thought a great deal about and one that I have not taken lightly. It is the right time. **"**

SIR ALEX FERGUSON

on retirement, May 2013

CHAPTER 7

THE GLORY DAYS

" George Best has ice in his veins, warmth in his heart and timing and balance in his feet. **"**

DANNY BLANCHFLOWER

❝You could knock the worst pass ever to Sparky and he would rip people's necks off to get it. At the time he wouldn't make gestures to make you look stupid, but a while later he'd come up to you and say, 'If you give me another pass like that, I'll have yer!'**❞**

PAUL PARKER

on the "the best all-round footballer I played with" – Mark Hughes

❝It makes me cringe just thinking about it. To this day, I have never watched a video of that game.**❞**

JIM LEIGHTON

remembers his calamitous performance in the 1990 FA Cup Final,
when United drew 3–3 with Crystal Palace and he was replaced by
Les Sealey in the replay, which United won 1–0

"The lads used to call me 'The Judge' because I sat on the bench so much.**"**

LES SEALEY

"Over the years people called several players the new Duncan Edwards… first Dave Mackay, then Bryan Robson. But none of them came close. He was the only player who ever made me feel inferior.**"**

SIR BOBBY CHARLTON

"Robbo was coming to the
end of his career when I joined United,
but I still got a sense of how important he
was at the club. He was a top player and just
to play with him towards the end of his
career was an honour.**"**

ROY KEANE

on legendary midfielder Bryan Robson

❝In my playing days, you had
confrontations but the whole team
didn't pile in with their handbags. I think
football's become a game of prima donnas.
I like watching rugby where players get stuck
into each other, but they just get up and get
on with it. **❞**

GEORGE BEST

bemoans modern players' behaviour

❝ Even when we played Leyton Orient away, there were 18,000 in the ground and more locked out. The crowds at home were great, but we really noticed it away because each game was a sell-out. That gave us a boost. It made us feel everyone was pulling together. **❞**

SAMMY McILROY

on fans' support in the 1974–75 season when United were promoted from Division Two

"In Turin, Gentile was marking me and I remember trying to get a cross in and he just stood on my shin. Later on, I was waiting for a corner and Gentile pulled a hair from under my armpit. I'd never had that before."

Former United winger **STEVE COPPELL**
recalls his painful lesson in the Italian art of defending during
United's 1978 UEFA Cup tie against Juventus

"When we won the Premiership in 1999, Dwight Yorke lifted the trophy and the crown fell off. I was in the crowd and turned to a total stranger and said: 'Great! I'll have to get that fixed on Monday!' She looked at me as though I was a total madman.**"**

Manchester United Museum curator **MARK WYLIE**

❝Anyone that witnessed what George could do on the pitch wished they could do the same. He made an immense contribution to the game, and enriched the lives of everyone that saw him play. It is a very sad day.**❞**

SIR BOBBY CHARLTON

marks the passing of George Best in November 2005